ANSWERING THE RUINS

ALSO BY GREGORY FRASER

Strange Pietà

Writing Poetry: Creative and Critical Approaches
(with Chad Davidson)

Answering the Ruins

POEMS

GREGORY FRASER

TRIQUARTERLY BOOKS • NORTHWESTERN UNIVERSITY PRESS • EVANSTON, ILLINOIS

TriQuarterly Books
Northwestern University Press
www.nupress.northwestern.edu

Printed in the United States of America

10 9 8 7 6 5 4 3 2

Library of Congress Cataloging-in-Publication Data

Fraser, Gregory.
    Answering the ruins : poems / Gregory Fraser.
       p. cm.
    ISBN 978-0-8101-2557-5 (pbk. : alk. paper) —
    ISBN 978-0-8101-2556-8 (cloth : alk. paper)
    I. Title.
   PS3606.R423A83 2009
   813.6—dc22

                                             2008031081

♾ The paper used in this publication meets the minimum requirements
of the American National Standard for Information Sciences—
Permanence of Paper for Printed Library Materials, ANSI Z39.48-1992.

THIS BOOK IS DEDICATED TO MARION FORD FRASER.

CONTENTS

3

4

Several of the poems in this collection appeared originally in the following journals:

American Literary Review: "The Other Side"

Arkansas Review: "The Discoverer," "The Present Moment"

Birmingham Poetry Review: "Charon's Sister," "Movers"

Chattahoochee Review: "Blood," "Stubble"

Chicago Review: "Scurvy"

Cimarron Review: "Assateague," "Ben's Apple"

Colorado Review: "Genesis of Henry Moore"

Green Mountains Review: "Summer Party Without Mark Strand," "Unmemoriam"

Hayden's Ferry Review: "Review of *The Selected Works of Stray Dog*"

Iron Horse Literary Review: "Poem for First Fathers"

Passages North: "Construction," "Gaul," "Goat," "Pussy"

Ploughshares: "Silverfish"

Poetry East: "Essay on Criticism," "Off Broadway," "Trophies Golden Trophies"

Subtropics: "Hephaestus Calls My Brother Home"

Sycamore Review: "Age of Reason"

Tampa Review: "Bisouxxx: A Brief Taxonomy," "Canticles"

Terminus: "Janus," "Jason"

Texas Review: "Fat"

32 Poems: "Hold"

Western Humanities Review: "Cheat," "Lot"

"Construction" was reprinted in the poetry anthology *Under the Rock Umbrella,* edited by William Walsh (Macon, Ga.: Mercer University Press, 2006).

"Miles" appeared in *A Different Bother,* an online chapbook published by Beard of Bees Press (Chicago, 2008).

I wish to thank my parents and my wife, Milada, for their constant encouragement and love. I am deeply grateful for the support of relatives, friends, and mentors, most notably Eric Elshtain, David Hartley, Jane Hill, Edward Hirsch, Susannah Mintz, and Robert Phillips. My greatest appreciation goes to Chad Davidson and Robert Hill for their companionship and poetic guidance. I would also like to thank the University of West Georgia and the National Endowment for the Arts.

ANSWERING THE RUINS

THE PRESENT MOMENT

Sometimes all it takes is a work whistle
clearing its dusty throat, or the scent of green
bananas, or a dropped fly ball, to start you

feeling sorry for the present moment, seated
at a bar in Pascagoula or Biloxi, lost
in gauzy ambivalence, hazed in smoke.

She sips her cocktail perfectly mixed—
equal parts heady future and currant-heavy
past—a drink that goes by the name

Radiant Equanimity or Insouciant Fire.
And all you want in the instant and instance
she is is to take in your hands her face—

tight as a surgeon's glove, droopy
as a waxen mask—and gaze at the twinkle
of one eye, the other's dying coal.

Because you know it has to be there:
the story of our being being told
by a jabbering Sphinx to some Scheherazade,

by stones to a current-laced stream—
our tale of sleeping in doorways of sleet,
swathed in mink. You want to lean in

to the present moment, profess your love
in every tongue she comprehends.
Ya lyublyu tebya, you'd whisper,

if Russian, *Ti amo,* if raised in Rome,
though you understand she lives
devoid of ardor, so we might not—

she, who is only fervor's reflection
in the mirror of her face, the very face
pressed now, right now, to your own.

1

CHEAT

Hang-ups in the dead of night,
and after training ourselves to unplug
before bed, crank calls at chance
hours throughout the week. We didn't want

to stir up conflict, hassle with running
a trace, and spent the summer waiting
for one lunacy to run its course. Then,
after the towers crumbled, nothing.

My wife had failed a finance major,
ruining his plan to graduate that May.
Appeals (apologetic, cajoling) gave way
to threats of litigation against our school.

I didn't know I could still run, an old man,
cloaked in dust, coughed to a TV crew,
awed by his breathless luck. And still I see
my twenty freshmen on that campus hill

in Queens, pleased with their release
from "Tintern Abbey," then stunned
by the twin smokes climbing.
My wife the Miltonist refused to budge,

pointing out the all too obvious
in the senior's copied essay. It was late
October before we noticed the calls
had stopped, and didn't he complain

of losing an internship downtown?
In our agnostic way—half-conscious,
tinged with the self-parodic—we prayed
that this *whining cheat* with his *sense of entitlement*

hadn't burned or been crushed by rubble.
He did have a pleasant smile, and was his crime
really such a disgrace? We watched the clock,
kept ears pricked over toast and coffee,

until he nearly became the son we never had,
whose memory needed tending. Who's to say
our number, all along, wasn't picked at random
by a lonesome freak who simply quit one day?

Still, neither of us dared to mention what I shrieked
one August night (rabid, moon in my eye): *Die,*
you little shit, assuming his to be the hostile
silence on the opposite end of the line.

PUSSY

That's what the guys back home would call me
if I climbed some Friday night onto a stool
at Sullivan's Tap Room, and started in
with how I want to be more accepting, permeable—
a nighttime sky, luminescence seeping through its holes.

The half-moon floats, mothlike, above the trees,
and I'm not sure why I stand on the porch alone,
thinking about these men. Hundreds of miles away, they curl
above their beers, less like the question marks their futures
have become, or the claw ends of hammers they grip all day,

pulling up shingles, yanking nails—and more like the gorgeous,
menacing waves of Hokusai, an artist I could never reference
without being taunted, *Wimp,* or jeered into buying
a round. Especially if I took a swig and started to jaw
about his "pictures of the floating world" school of printmaking,

the curves that dazzled Monet—or worse, if I glossed
my half-drunk buddies' *wimp,* how it captures the coward
crouched and shivering inside every pretentious display.
If I ever told Dave Soley I love him, he'd mutter *queer,*
maybe beat my ass. Still, I wish I'd held him like a brother

the night he sobbed for his brother, returned unscathed
from Vietnam to blow the jungle from his mind.
Go long, Bill Singley barked, pigskin in hand, so I ran
until I crossed the nation, sat in class with the liquid vowels
of Dylan Thomas, Delmore Schwartz. Meanwhile,

my friends ran trowels across cement, which means they'd stare
like I'd gone nuts if I voiced my admiration for the limping
garden mad with clouds, rivers thrashing in March.
Could I lilt to them my sissy aches: refusing to spell
my mother's hair, its tilt to the fragile, or trying to pull

my youngest brother's voice, Excalibur, from his body's stone,
while seeking to match him, alone for alone? Perhaps
they'd pat my back, say how much it matters to have a pal
not only thinking up this crap but writing it down. Or one
might rise from his swiveled stool, chant his own pussiness:

Our species mumbles in the future's ear. I, Vince Cerio,
doubt clear words but believe in wonders from dusk to dawn
that keep us speaking. All bones end in a flaming word,
though we gleam like fevers, thrust onto heartlands, marry lament.
At closing time, last call, we yield to elders, sing to ancient winds.

The Phils lead 4 to 2. *The Breaking Wave Off Kanagawa*
may be Hokusai's greatest work. Who cares? I only know
it isn't rootlessness but roots bereft of soil that makes me
want to hug my oldest friends tonight, as shingled roofs
up and down my block drive wedges between the stars.

POETRY IS STUPID

I was majoring in dendrology and girls,
failing both, so when my hated roommate
burst in from English class, slammed
down his book bag, and declared, *Poetry
is stupid—it does nothing for the world,*

I knew I'd found my calling. One
look at his composition, scrawled in red
like a field at Maldon, I smirked and hit
the stacks, came back loaded down:
Milton, Dickinson, Auden, Rich.

He whined for days, calling the teacher
idiot, bitch, recounting his unbroken string
of high-school As. *Ou sont les neiges d'antan?*
I despised his loafers, Izod shirts, smooth
persuasion of hair, and envied with a numbing ache

the queue of beauties he ushered in, cueing me,
with a nod, to beat it. I'd slump off
to the Student Center, pore through "Howl,"
Homeric Hymns, repeating the mantra
beneath my breath, *Poetry is stupid* . . .

Second term, I traded *Pinus nigra*
for Robert Frost, *Catalpa speciosa*
for Sexton and Plath. And slowly, as middle
Pennsylvania thawed, the notebooks filled:
Tonight, I lose my birth weight in sweat

alone, sip the matter of my fall in rye,
chew the cattle's flesh, spin like a spider
the lace of verse . . . Recitation
vexed the jerk—*Cut that shit,* he'd snap
from his annexed two-thirds of our space.

Rumor has it he made a killing
in the dot-com boom. They say
he even clanged the bell one morning
at the stock exchange—gross tintinnabulations.
In my mind's eye, though, I place him

in a smaller scene, purchasing a birthday
gift for his wife (the third). He browses
down the wrong aisle in a Barnes & Noble,
and spotting my name along one spine,
double-takes and says out loud: *Hey,*

I roomed with that hand-job freshman year.
Then he cracks the slender volume, peruses
till he finds the poem—this poem—dedicated
to none other than him: my adversary,
my antonym, my Unferth, my muse.

FAT

The dolts in Shipping & Receiving called her . . . I'll let you guess.
Payday, ten to five, she asked me out in a sentence that lurched
like a car sputtering out of gas, cozying up to a midnight curb—

but trust me, it wasn't that kind of date. I felt sorry for her, a little
contrite about feeling sorry, sick of staring into my Sylvania's flat,
black-and-white face, and hungry for change, if not Italian,

in hex-sign-riddled middle Pennsylvania, which she proposed.
Heels that proved her novice, overrouged, a shawl the same
diluted pink of the house rosé, and I remember talking while we ate

about the company's outsize share in floor and ceiling tile,
about the fat Christmas bonuses that never of course appeared
on our well-below-middle-management desks.

I might have mentioned the poems I was writing after hours
(okay, during)—poems rotten beyond revision.
May they bloom mold and go down in the suck of time,

since I'd just as soon forget those first inchoate years
writing PR and in-house ads, wearing worsted suits
and a thin blue mask of computer light in a cubby hole

the length and width of a pullout bed—but again,
the night didn't go that way. She paid cash, left too fat a tip,
and suggested a walk through town. I paused, then said,

Why not? Be patient. I'll explain why not soon enough.
A poem must receive before it gives adequate pause.
For now, picture her arms, braided across an ample chest,

and me holding hands with myself behind my back.
We pass a darkened Auto Parts, a grocery store
out of Hopper, and now she steers us to a jeweler's glass

to gaze at financeable dazzle—guarded by a chubby,
cuddly, idiot-eyed teddy bear dressed in a beefeater suit,
YOUR FREE GIFT WITH THE PURCHASE OF ANY DIAMOND.

It's there she asks if I've thought of marriage, swearing
she'll never wed before I stammer an answer. A band
of frat boys—ball caps, untied sneaks—sniggers past, and the night

begins to eddy at our ankles, calves. The silence begs a *Why?*
and I give my paltry alms, receiving more than my overpriced B.A.
prepared me for, about the real American Gothic. She describes

the megastore that drove her father's hardware under,
how he took to driving his voice into her mom.
I listen mutely, careful not to harm with platitude.

Slowly, her mother hardened, until tenderness meant
the bruising on her upper arms where he grabbed
and shook her once, before vanishing out West.

That's wrong. I was careful, thoughtful, of nothing then.
I stood speechless because the distance in her voice
was haunting, because all at once I thought I understood

why *missing* means both *absent* and the short-of-breath,
galumphing work left over when something loved is lost.
Huge clouds reclined above the streetlamps, Ingres nudes.

I must have stretched a hand, placed it on her shoulder,
or maybe shifted my feet, but something caused her to turn
abruptly, stare into my eyes, and say I was a handsome,

talented fraud, and she knew of nothing sadder
than the inauthentic. She told me she despised the way
I swaggered down the halls, talking football in Sales,

flirting with the temps. She hated that most, she said—
not out of envy for them, but for me, someone so
insipidly carefree. It was over before I could interrupt,

mount my thin defense. A candy wrapper tumbled past.
A motorcycle slit open a distant street. She lowered her eyes,
apologized. I said I was sorry, too, just then feeling

the urge to kiss her, but only asked to walk her home.
We stopped at the whitewashed gate, fence slats
shining like broadswords under the moon.

Thanks, she said, and we both leaked out a laugh
that died touching the air. Then she climbed,
gracefully removing her shoes first, the stair.

CHARON'S SISTER

In bed that night after the clinic, after the bearded man
in the parking lot waved his placard, named you *Jezebel,*
killer bound for hell, I ranted—a zealot—about the gall
of zealots, all temerity and jutting noses, and wanted
to bust his lip, split into shards that loveless sign.

You leaned over and kissed my brow, its three-line stanza
of consternation, then described a vacant feeling, high
in your chest, rocking like an empty seat, you said,
at the top of a Ferris wheel. When I think back to our affair,
a sadness seizes and releases me. Likewise a joy.

Thirty-five to my twenty-four, you dreamed out loud
of good fools like us, making their lives the love
of their lives. You said you desired the knotty unanimity
of outer space, with its declaration of one vast sentence
eternally extended by ellipses of light. No, that's me

trying not to sound prosaic. You would have used
one earthly image—the Ferris wheel, for instance,
at a county fair, just when quaintness seemed most needed,
most absurd. This evening, watching constellations
beat like moths against the screen, I am still unable

to love that man, though my journal states:
You can love the righteous as you do the rose,
being neither. That night (has it now been twenty years?)
I expected to dream of fires into which he meant
to cast us—of Dante's Ferris wheels inside Ferris wheels,

toppled, ablaze. Instead, the pagan underworld
swirled up, a woman in a narrow punt
working a pole through murk. She wore your face.
On the shore, a figure clad in shadow clutched a sign
that you, bearing an unborn passenger, refused to read.

AUTOBIOGRAPHY AT SEVENTEEN

My father kept harping on some crazy train
hauling or somehow fueled by gravy
and scheduled to shriek to a halt

sooner than I could conjure. Then I'd be holding
what his baritone—freighting the word
with consequence—called

The Bag. What filled this mystery sack?
The weight of a world named manhood?
A secret formula of drippings and roux,

magically able to make stuck iron
locomotive—zany with travel,
according to my high-school Spanish?

And he never let up on the draft,
though Vietnam had passed, and my best
friend's brother returned home safe

to blast out his brains. Like most,
I loved my father too much to tell him,
and knew no way to break my simple want

to his butcher's block, chestnut stump,
back-shed anvil of a heart. *To write?*
About what, son, what? I didn't know,

for years, but behind my eyes I watched
the long steel stems of rail lines bloom
into cities spiked with headquarters, hotels,

central stations. I could hear but not yet mimic
kingfishers, grackles, wrens—every one
a Socrates, writing nothing down.

My father constructed a house of cautions.
I couldn't recline for long, he warned,
in a mythic catbird seat: too dangerous

a vantage. Someone was always glad
to promote my ruin, with a mouth
forever thirsting, despite the facial calm.

Too soon, nurses with a common smile
will survey his heart—a green horizon
spiked with forty mountains per minute.

On one, a spider tends its lines, another darts
with deer I chase down wooded paths.
About loss, father, of course, about the distances

between us, which account for all our shouting
in spaces tight as private compartments,
where travelers open lunches in crinkled bags,

hoping to find a tuna on rye transformed
into a hot meal slathered with gravy
perfectly seasoned, in strangely abundant supply.

HEPHAESTUS CALLS MY BROTHER HOME

for Jonathan, 1970–2004

He kissed the concave oxygen, felt the silver punch,
    and at the laying on of paddles, jolted as if reborn.
        As it was early morning—America is gone—he tore

down streets in A-lines, through automatic glass,
    into anesthesia, vertiginous and gauzy. My brother
        entered the scalpel's edge, sky-watt bulb, voices

by hygiene muffled, but not before potassium
    stunned his heart. He rolled to the holding parlor,
        swept into and swiftly out of sympathy cards—

mawkish, embossed, posted from many states.
    And he slipped beneath bouquets, omega phrases
        of our father, who dreamily once believed

nothing could stop our healing in bandages of wine,
    nothing negate the seven original wonders:
        those holes in heads where worlds stream in.

Don't conjure any Hermes, pinion-footed,
    or Apollo in spiky luminescence. At the hour
        of my brother's birth, Hephaestus hobbled

out of hunchbacked woods, raised a shield
    that bore a contorted likeness. Tender he
        crouched at the nurse door. And at my brother's parting,

Vulcan held the mask, veered the screeching wagon.
    An ambulance called my brother's name,
        and with his crippled creator, he wheeled away,

leaving the strict dress code of orchids,
  the partridge in pasture, declining the bullet's offer.
    My brother left boulders to kneel in prayer,

rains to rinse away all but the faces
  of prophets, printed on rattlesnake coils.
    Spastically, he waved farewell to books

unread, lamps with umbilicals fused to walls.
  He disappeared from priests with golden
    anchors about their necks, from bakers who,

gloved in flour, recall Victorian spinsters.
  And alone, breadless, in a fog like shadow,
    I wandered prairies of cereal and steel,

gravel patches, and white-sand beaches—
  chalk outlines of murdered islands.
    I ignored the parachutes of blossoms

packed inside spring buds, fell deaf to April
  leaching through the sieves of poplars,
    lindens' yellow seines. And once as I strayed

thinking, his hair gleamed river dark.
  Hunting the hind love, only movement meaning,
    I hated the good luck stamped on my red and white

blood shields, hated Halloweeners, who knocked
  at my brother's gate, mocked his crook,
    hitch and hook. Release the face, Hephaestus.

I am my faith in talking. I am days interior,
  up against the night, drowsing in a single want.
    I need a nest, a sight, I need to meet the twilight

branching, where red plums go for twenty, and whispers
        outearn the bellow. Say something, anvil stalker.
                Every cell block wants its speech, with rust in the rose

and babble of tellings. But the clubfoot wouldn't
        budge, and all that time my brother loved his work—
                founding wheels, forging frames for all his kind.

He relished what he could not fashion
        in the factories of his first. Let me enter
                a sapling's cure, green branches slender as sleet,

trunks still learning how to count their rings.
        As dawn spotlights for losses (the mouse undone,
                the rabbit taken) my wit is dewy bright. Split

my brother, Hephaestus—half to you, half
        for me. And still the gimpy maker clutched.
                I wished on an empty sky, on storms

when lightning locks horns with oak.
        I tied stones to keep from shaking,
                spent afternoons at the corner pub,

watching locals saunter in, stumble out.
        What happened to the laughter strong as rye?
                I made no money, nor love, nor weeping,

and far from the ground sores
        of our parents' passing, I hardly pictured
                my one lit window in the final house.

I followed instead the moon not round
        but crescent, not period but comma. And true
                as any ambulance shrieks a brother gone,

Hephaestus refused once more, pointing
　　　　with mangled index at my brother's eye, joyful
　　　　　　as he tightened bolts, worked the villanelles

of wing nuts, fit precisely the padded seats.
　　　　I should have moved to Birmingham,
　　　　　　with its largest cast-iron statue in the world,

should have forgone the salts of my days,
　　　　embraced the bringers of sickness
　　　　　　and the grubby kine. I drew up resolutions then:

I will not count my shabby possessions
　　　　nor part with them. I will know the dead
　　　　　　are not enough to hold. I'll walk no street

that sneers at birthmarks. Search for water,
　　　　I will, with my clavicles' divining rod.
　　　　　　I will read by the backbone's little bulbs,

and not imagine my destined hour
　　　　pausing, deerlike, midstride. I'll seek
　　　　　　asylum in the word, not fret about its mazes.

And strive by barely knowing. I will pass through
　　　　gray light into summer, and teach the clock
　　　　　　another walk, truer to its one foreshortened limb.

Again, the ironworker dismissed.
　　　　So I denounced my brother's founder.
　　　　　　And soon, my curse was answered.

He who never took one step rolled to me
　　　　with small allotment, and no upgrade
　　　　　　to his form. He wheeled gray-brown, animal coated,

where snowfall sculpts the busts of fire hydrants,
and *Once* keeps red its coal. Once, we were innocence
in wetness bonded, answering the ruins.

And we began for chance, guessing our way
to under-people and sidewalks rampless.
East, the mica-ed pavements winked. We followed

their come-hithers, our swift farewell
an ancient trick up the river's silk.
Pretending he'd been kidnapped, together

we pulled up—to prevent our being tracked—
the stitching down centers of two-lane roads.
We spoke with migrant lip, gliding from town

to town, kissing everybody's language.
We studied atlases on the backs of well-formed
hands and ill. And as we supposed our passage,

my brother's head was fair, forever,
storing the spiders' nets, the cherry's bone—
how gentle of you, Jon. We guessed the oldest

and the toll. And I knew the whole world wanders,
awestruck, through its changes. Even the inanimate
crawls: rust on a nail. There is nothing to favor

in balance. Why honor gods who covet?
An ambulance howled my brother's name,
and like a king snake feeding, the river swelled.

So we surmised our way past oil derricks,
tireless fornicators, a slope with Hapsburg lip.
We skirted highway interchanges, keeping

the land in full and half nelsons. Our mood was fruit.
       All that hulking softness is gone. Long
             streets delivered strangers—some historians,

leading with the past to stave off doom,
       others futurists, who feared the rearing of daughters
             with legs lengthy as catcalls. We met very few

who oil the here and now. Say *there,* say *still.*
       I feel possessive as an ocean, grasping
             graveled sands to retrieve its dead.

And Hephaestus showed too soon to thieve
       my brother home. There must be suppertimes
             in an upper world. Cottages hung

on hinges, and under a pine's soft rattle,
       beneath that high anointment, my brother
             in disease passed back to the root.

2

SILVERFISH

Pressed between print, haunting gutters, we traded closeness
for dialogue and plot, dropped concordantly to sleep

not long before dawn, hardbacks propped on our chests
like tents on a plain in Cooper. Wingless, piscatorial,

we dined on starches and molds, slid into cracks, crevices,
bathtubs on occasion. Troubled to escape their slick,

enameled palisades, we chose the horizontal: *Leaves of Grass*
in lounge chairs by the pool, Ginsberg on blow-up rafts.

Our rooms, bibliographic amphitheaters, thronged
with titled spines. *The Odyssey, The Frogs, Selected Poems*

by John Crowe Ransom. We burrowed in Woolf,
gnawed Updike and Austen, all of whom declared,

The first sorrow can be lifted but not hauled off—
a theme we paid too little notice, paying ransom to it,

as we were, for and with our lives. During famine,
we attacked the leatherware: fine-bound collector's copies.

Naturally, we considered children nymphs, creatures
of liquid and myth. A decade's passed since last

we kissed. Were we mistaken to embrace,
or simply overtaken by aversions to the real?

One time, in a viscid afternoon no one but us recalls,
I climbed the broken back of a sweet-gum tree

while you snapped photos, unmindful of your thumb
obscuring the lens. One can block a part of the heart,

you know. You know, *Lepisma saccharina,*
sweet tooth, old friend of sizing and glue. Thankfully,

the damage we did, commensurate with our kind,
was slight—minor foxing of silks and rayon.

Yet I sometimes think we might have flourished
had we canoed the Susquehanna, or submitted

to the balms of church. Studious, antennae raised,
we sought protection in exacted meaning, forced

our minds to mind and called the act *reflection.*
It didn't help. Lost in leitmotifs, humidities

of simmering conflict, we came to begrudge
the characters we consumed—their crafted shapeliness,

perfect aim at fate. Who could blame us in our supple
exoskeletons, lank appendages? We had to part.

Like every paradise, ideal companionship exists purely
on the page, is the page. Here. For old times. Feed on this.

OFF BROADWAY

I loved a woman who cherished orchids less
than weeds, gray-headed dandelions running off
with the wind to seed. Adoring what let her in,
as I did not, she suspected the concave-convex
manner of the sea: blue invitations offered
then withdrawn. I still turn corners in cities
we tramped—Kyoto, Edinburgh—hoping to crash
in her hair. With a single lesson, like a cloud,
her hair could speak the native wind (scirocco,
breeze-over-the-dale) wherever our loved grants
landed us. If only our shadows, one long afternoon,
could cross in a truce without our knowing.
Somewhere off Broadway make it, near the first apartment
we rented, for what seems now like next to nothing.

CONSTRUCTION

In the dog fact and catch of the matter,
something must hold true outside the jungle,
one old error we might correct. I slouched
in a pub downtown, handcuffed by my wristwatch
to the stool. Had someone given a crisp
reproach, my fingers might have mended
the boggling sameness. Truthfully, I never took
to Boston, where we gradually wore on,
then into, one another—our wishes mourning
the calendar's grid. But I always liked
our talk of canyons, and the hard *somehow*
of vintage pinups. Let high air gnaw
at heaven's crossbeams. Today, I remove
another wildness from my résumé, refuse to listen
when neighbors' squabbles crosshatch the morning.
A man hacks loudly at the end of the bar.
The dull street sighs outside, its curbs too still.
Right here, you would have said, *let's build.*

GAUL

Among hunting dogs, packs are always counted
in couples, while a hare is said to be *balled up*
when its feet become *clay clogged.* Had I stayed—
forced with you to recount the lovely thens,
before the burden of forgetting broke us—
how in the plush Algonquin could our notion
of the lobby further ornament that space?
I learned with you to avoid the questions
glinting like trumpets, in favor of the one
in French-horn coils. Sixteen feet of metal tubing
tangle in that forlorn horn—a descendant
of the same *trompe de chasse* hunters blew
four centuries ago, pursuing the coy Reynard.
In any case, *you and I* became a pat expression,
a set of instructions to ourselves and friends,
while all along the rules were the only players,
arranging us like game pieces carved of wood
or horn (as with the first blown horns).
Keep the money heavy as flagstone. Buy
tickets to *Die Walküre,* your favorite opera,
though Wagner vexed the Russian Jew in you.
It would have been nice to find America together,
instead of reading by slow black windows.
Yet I pity us less than the clarinetist
with all that brass behind her like family wealth
or the loud mistake she surely made one summer,
hunting for ardor in a country once called Gaul.

GOAT

You haven't lived if you haven't screamed, at least once, like a bullet,
and lodged in a Muscovite's chest. Nine hundred miles away
in Syracuse, the nation's cloudiest city, my fiancée refuses to talk dirty

over the phone, believing the KGB will brand us shameless—
net styda. The wall's down how many years? In Glenside, Queens,
where we first met, flight paths thatched the sky, cemeteries

(the first rock gardens) bloomed, and I thought of my first wife,
of the third finger of the left hand, which is only the first part
forced through gold. I know it's foolish playing the hunchback now,

worshipping a simple wonder. *But to live on lilaced streets,*
breathing feminine time. History, you amputee, let me touch
your phantom leg, bring back the night the goat escaped

and I heard old castles crumble. Almost dusk, miles
from then, the distance out my window opens its gardenia.
I should play some Sarah Vaughan. There's a woman who knew

two stones reside in every stone. I lift the receiver instead,
dial clouds, remembering that splotch on Gorbachev's skull,
Yeltsin in tennis shorts. To M——, their faces are breaths

on winter glass. Lucky there's still talk clear as pianos.
That's how we learn who hails from a drinking family,
who sees the river of noon swimming in bights of twilight.

BLOOD

All day, my wife-to-be draws threads of AB negative, B positive, O,
sewing the admitted back to Sunday suppers, Bob Barker, and Barcaloungers.

Tonight, brash as neon, she asks me to marry her mother, unable in Samarkand
to charm the U.S. consulate. The fat last fly of autumn lolls

on the window ledge. The fridge lets out a sigh. Pre-me, before escaping,
my fiancée delivered Uzbeks, preemies mostly, coaxed with a slap their cries,

held their almost lifeless lightness. *It's done,* she insists, *all the time.*
You divorce in months, like nothing. Blue among beeps, clotted hellos,

patients in ICU praise my future wife, quickest to find the vein.
Why then can't she see: books grow restless on my lap, and every period

prophecies the death of reading? An us ago, I clutched steel-haired guitars
and sang. Loneliness built a scarecrow of my name, frightened off contentment—

glossy and passerine—which was part of what I crooned. Later,
through static, I first talked to her mother. She spoke of banks refusing

withdrawals, women threatened with veils. Knowing only seven words of Russian,
I heard: *Before was a wonder road, the day of the sparrow never passed.*

Then mountains opened blouses, like bypass patients, and showed the scars.
In college, a B was beyond negative. I'd raise a paw, repeat that "Tintern Abbey"

is a *descriptive-meditative crisis autobiography,* but fail to read
the cold blue winds of late November. I can't be positive.

Darkness arrives as revelation—ancient, wooing—wiping from sight
the turquoise cupolas of the Registan, rotund fruit in bazaars I've yet to walk.

A year together, at most, my fiancée urges, *then you and I can wed.*
Her English could not be better. I hear: *Hold out your arm, I've come for blood.*

STUBBLE

Had my parents been alive or dead, I might not walk this middle kingdom,
where rivers ask with bluesy mouths the giant *Why?* of the sea.

I'm more or less what the bone recites. Nights, as my fiancée chirps long distance
to Brighton Beach, the Tallapoosa mothers its shattered moon.

I like a beard, she states at breakfast, *reminds me of home.* Does shaving mean
waffles cold, unbuttered? The old contraptions of self and other losing hold?

Men I grew up with, hours north, bulge about the beltline, thin at the scalp,
vanish into ethnic jokes, choruses of rye. They married young, I wavered—

having watched a groom collapse, crack his skull on marble. I have hummed
to family for years: *If I die, choose the gold death box and parlor of light.*

Give my papers to fire not wind. I need to stop trying on graves, just wear
my given clothes. Once, my signature inspired bellhops on the Upper East Side.

At her *pleeeeze,* I V-ed open shirts an extra button. Pond lilies, eight-armed
Shaktis, spread palms to light in Central Park. Did she, daughter of Himalayas,

think me foolish when I called all water bugs messiahs? I don't suggest
we open mouths, root for ancient words. But I admit: as we hunted Fifth

for pastries (*babka,* yeasty *vatrushki*), I felt a pleasant ache in my body's own
Upper East Side. Here, a knock on wood means *luck,* in Moscow, *stupid.*

Pressing lips to yesterdays, kissing what I knew—that's dumb no matter where.
My future wife stood over the bathroom sink this morning, uncharmed

by the converse galaxies there. Still, I'll follow friends back home
and wed unbearded, showing only the promise of hair.

THE OTHER SIDE

We may be living strangers' afterlives, all
of us darting about or lolling in what they call
the other side. No matter. Isn't it enough
to live in flotsam—smell of rough

wet wool, dusk, a ripened grape, you and I in the ticket
line, afraid again to bungle? Admit
the one wire holding me together
still divides us, thinly. You're right: we must be either

God's dream or vice versa—the one true beauty
not knowing which. Before we marry,
know this: someday my face
will open like the glass

cover of a mantel clock, and a slender hand will set me
to the proper instant. I cannot guarantee
yours will be that hand, only that earth
forgives our nastiness—its sediment (worth

millions) kindly forgetting outside Tucson—
the very setting of this action
thriller, judging by the cacti and highway's drone
scored on power lines. Soon,

at five times twenty miles per hour,
our twenty-foot heroes of light will soar
over a cliff. Into what? Us?
The ghosts of our fictive casualties? Know this

as well before we vow: in cineplexes, I pay less
attention to the film than to its watchers. Studious
as mirrors, eyeballs flash, eager
to let the next death enter.

BISOUXXX: A BRIEF TAXONOMY

Close-lipped kisses wander sooner than French,
while Eskimo appear less apt than vacuum
(kissing openmouthed, drawing another's air)
to recall the cities' invitations, each road longing
for more thoroughfare, fewer shoulders.

Early October, breath blooming gray
at an open window, I drank to expand the mind
like a frame of film in a faulty projector—
Bogart and Hepburn, say, in silhouette, melting.
Once, my front teeth clamped one half

of a Russian chocolate, and a woman from Samarkand
stole the other with her mouth. Outside the small café,
a fat sun kept its only word, and I knew, divorced,
I'd never make it eating or cleaning, even pissing alone,
unsure if my rooms were asleep or wakeful.

Gently work an earlobe, one text instructs. *Avoid
loud sucking noises.* Forget what these books neglect:
that nights are different a little south, laden
with embankments, ice cubes exchanged by tongues.
How long had I dwelt in rafters, spitting grape seeds

from a fire escape as stairways leaped from floor
to floor and clothes-lined blouses hovered
between ghost and flesh? *With faces a breath
apart, open and close your eyelids
against a partner's.* The *butterfly,* it's called.

Done correctly, they say, *the fluttering sensation
matches the one in your heart.* But I believe in
an absolute heart, guarded by under-folk. Where Broadway
and Seventh kiss, for instance, an indigent sprawls
beneath a late marquee flashing xxx . . . xxx . . . xxx.

JANUS

I envy children staring through their peepholes,
unaware of bodies as form-fitted cells, of birth
as the latest breakthrough in incarceration.

Twin-tongued, I urge them not to gulp the last
glassfuls of laughter. Can you recite the word
we conjured for sham embraces? Surely

someone awash in understanding recollects,
not fooled by the wires of winter branches
electric with dawn. I'm doubly entranced by you,

and thank the constellations, grasses ironed flat
by wind. So what if the copper moon recalls
summers penniless, loaves verdigrised with mold.

Half of you compels me to forgive,
instead of clutching rails, howling at the sea.
The other insists on my presenting

a garland of long-stemmed islands, rooted
to the ocean floor, blooming above the tides.
They say madness skips away, stone

across a pond. Where it sinks, no one fathoms.
Elsewhere, someone sits in meditation,
keeping the common heart from drifting off.

Mine, by contrast, bends: I stagger toward the pines.
Suppose the spring stops barging in,
reannouncing essential good. Say the walls

dissolve then reappear—thicker, windowless.
This city once was lit by velvet gods, and I watched
your eyeballs rustle beneath their sheets.

Better madness than an unnamed pain.
So vanish if you must. No, stay.
Here comes the daybreak, here the evening star.

LOT

When the world was a smaller mistake,
I counted the mercy stones, but now read ruin
into all creation as jealous husbands sense escape

in the most mundane of a wife's departures.
Will your body be my last? Am I designed to quaver
each time fast-food neon flashes *Shakes*?

You were correct: a genuine blunder
is worthy of stuffing, flanked with cornbread,
cranberry-and-pineapple chutney.

Isn't it marvelous what we weren't
an eon ago—naked on a corner, beeped at
by cabs? Still, old covenants can't keep evenings

afloat, or the moon on its humped migration,
though the table looks lovely tonight,
its candles' thin wax pillars

throwing our doubles on the walls.
Would you kindly pass the salt?
This history could stand a pinch.

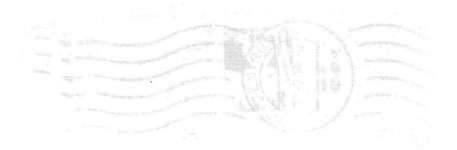

3

AGE OF REASON

Your rent's past due, pants untidy
on hangers, and no wife hunts for letters
ensconced in sock drawers. With us, everyone

is at least his double, her own half self.
Whistles from balconies drift, smokelike,
fall to water branching in fire. Here: Cadillac,

with the North Star system, automatic locks.
There: Condillac, the good atheist, his *Treatise on Sensations*,
of which you approved. We too dream of angels

pledging to die in wrecks, to enter the un-noise
gripping a clammy bone. So much so we barely notice
the sea colors of bruises—sudden as a marble patio

after French doors open. Your falling off must
have pierced like trumpets, until the Romantics
appeared, their hearts wandering coasts,

fumbling driftwood. *Realism, Analysis, Ideology:*
other ages stack like chips in poker—the game
derived from the eighteenth century's *poque.*

Today, I call your bluff, raise you a fever curling
from oatmeal, two clams casino, and my next-door neighbor
whose husband beat her blonde, then black and blue,

as you did the Middle Ages. She came lonely
as a floorboard, asked for help with the rent.
We stretched on a cot, my pants pouring over a chair

like . . . no, *our comparisons are vague,*
as Condillac insisted, *causing us to shift attention
from one object to another.* These gravestones,

for instance, which will never say
they're sorry, these ants, knowing no date,
peering past our soirées to somewhere holy.

Étienne Bonnot is gone, and we must choose among the dead
buried in love, those cast underground in spite,
those converted with admiration to ash, others spilled

into oceans. This takes time, three centuries or more.
Thankfully, the typewriter works all night,
tapping out the notice of your eviction.

ESSAY ON CRITICISM

It's hard not to think of yourself sometimes
as a passing mention in the dense
forgettable middle of a Russian novel,

as the brief description of a minor
character's gesture, the offhand reference
to a body of water, smell of rye bread.

The plot would falter without you,
the grand style momentarily flag,
but you could just as easily be scratched.

Still, you can't help seeing yourself
as the brash initial sentence, those ambiguous
final lines, or dialogue choked through sobs.

Perhaps it's not so awful to settle in
to a small remark on a peddler's
mule-drawn *voz,* glint off a samovar.

Then again, there's always the chance
of a critic (diligent, not unbeautiful)
prepared to make more of you

than any could imagine. In such a case—
you Aside, Casual Comment—propose
on the instant, latch on till The End.

HOLD

Lulled by Muzak, tempered plastic at the ear,
you neglect to study the eyes of fathers, ghosted
with cataracts, to read the moon from right

to left, like Hebrew. Imagine numbers you might
have wooed, held while Hold held you—lovers
demure as watermarks, aloof as china closets,

paramours in robes, in hordes, brandishing the curved
ribs of their births. Push 1 to proceed in English.
Dos en Español. 1's for mist, the first impressionist,

working *en plein air,* as you drum four fingers,
a plumper thumb. *Please hold,* the recording lilts.
Tenga por favor. Isn't this the first appeal

in every tongue? Don't infants screech it,
hurt friends sigh, those undone, alone?
So you've sanctified the towhee, which needs

no purification. So your flesh and blood
are hand-me-downs from your parents'
dated wardrobes. Press 3 to watch a blackbird

part the sky, half for heaven, half for the salty
grass of Brigantine, where the sun drives
terrible bargains. Behold Hold, in splendor,

granting time to roll a name's hard candy
on the tongue. Before long, you'll enter the scent
of lemons, sound of a faucet running.

Your spouse is washing dishes there, hair
in a comb-over or bun. On the radio, a country singer
croons: *I'd rather die than have you leave me,*

'cause losing you would kill me my whole life.
Push 4 for melodrama, 5 for cynicism,
6 for hay-bale curlers in the farmland's hair.

All day, you have been bounced from Hold
to Hold, and now they've come at last—
the words for which you've waited

what seems like your whole life:
Good afternoon, this is Tina. With whom
do I have the pleasure of speaking?

POEM FOR FIRST FATHERS

On the evening of the rasps and ululations,
when fever sings and singes your palm,
the rooftops of neighbors' houses turn
to the shingled skin of something restless, utterly
wrong, sliding across the top of your block.
Wind, rumpling the sheets of trees, is
no longer wind, and though the skies lack
thunder, rain, the power verges on blacking out.
Beside the crib where a child coughs,
wriggles in its own flame, you stare out
the six-paned window, convinced the quarter moon
is one of a pair of hooked incisors, just as surely
as you know you've conjured this massive
presence—famished, bereft of time—
rubbing the side of its face on glass.
Your wife, exhausted, dreams an infant
adrift on a Nile of fire. She is unable to sense
the weighty motions of what would be too pat
to name a serpent, despite the crocodile musk
in your nose. Nor can she hear the start
of a bargain between the father you've become
and the other you thought you renounced.
You swear to straighten up, apologize
to those you hurt, and drop to your knees
without forgetting a creature at once all muscle,
all brain, base and luminescent—scratching
itself on chimneys, settling houses
into foundations that might as well be sand
since your child is now a ball of winter,

a miniature Mars. That's when you want war
with that deadbeat in the heavens, His answers
regular as chance, but even more so with a force
that wears the armor of neighbors' roofs, bending
branches and bearing the moon, come to announce
itself and demand some tribute—a girl or boy
not one year old, or a poem where it appears
in glory, while a newborn struggles to sleep
and skies begin to crack with flashes of gills.

THE DISCOVERER

My great-grandfather believed in nothing
except his muskrat-toothed hammer,
with which he opened mail. He'd secret the tool
to bed, where it nibbled on his wife.

As a young man, my great-grandfather noticed
mirrors have no memories, and would have
invented the camera (so runs the story)
if it hadn't been for *cards 'n' hooch.*

Twilight kept pointing out the body
stashed in brambles on the family farm.
Only rigor mortis and a nursery
of maggots took the hints.

One night late, my great-grandfather packed
and left his family, only to drop
his rucksack scrambling back up the porch.
(Of course, he'd stumbled on

the threadbare corpse—one Molly P. of N.B.)
What the authorities didn't mutter:
Lilacs are not so hard of hearing as we suppose.
A good poem is like smelling salts. Etc.

Instead, their cameras flashed a mask of notoriety
on my great-grandfather's face,
which stared at me again this morning
through the yellowed pane of "his" clipping.

Oh, his dumb heart made a hobby
of grieving, when it might have learned
to whittle chessmen, collect matchbooks, tie flies.
Me? I possess his hammer and his name.

ASSATEAGUE

Debonair hunter of shorelines, white-tailed socialite
well appointed, the egret strangely calls to mind
a grade-school bruiser twice your size, half as clever,

averse to soap and reading. Like the moon,
the brain has phases: you must be crescent-minded now,
as a sliver connects the snowy flier, dining on crabs,

and a kid with knuckles sharp as angles
in geometry class. In the Gay Nineties, egret plumes adorned
a jaunty hat. Style, then as today, hastened extinction.

Yawning moons make waters yawn, and spring
through autumn, egrets light on Assateague.
That isn't why he beat you. He struck

because his brother pummeled him
because *his* father failed to rise and thrash *his* father,
whose father came home pissed and started swinging.

The crudeness of the egret's nest, its elliptical,
reptilian egg, suggest a place among the lower birds.
You signed your name in pee with his

one heavy snow, and even spent a summer night
at the bully's home. In sleep, he sucked his thumb.
Trapezoid, rhomboid, parallelogram:

you tried to bring him up to speed, but all he did
was stare through window glass at ghosts,
black-billed and yellow-footed.

TROPHIES GOLDEN TROPHIES

for the family at the end of the block
with the John Deere rider mower
the ice-cream maker for summer Sundays
when the moon drowns in its light

for years their firstborn murders her violin
hacking away and away
then packs two trunks for Julliard
trophies golden trophies

for the mother who bakes
father who lawyers in town
big sister who helps her brother with homework
trophies

for the simple prayers at supper
the nonmention of gravediggers
avoidance of nasty brawls
curse-spitting spats

it takes too long to learn
a door is merely a wall on hinges
it's too easy to forget to love the street prophets flashy as flamingos
their entire weight on the leg of one skinny truth

we have found the mud facedown
barely breathing
we have looked friendly but labored at giving
so trophies golden trophies

for the two-car garage and tidy tool bench
the flowered kitchen and its simple clock
which can count no higher than twelve
but still stays happy

true
front lawns cannot displace
the great screwup of the human
and destroyers never want for business

but golden trophies
for bird feeders stuffed with seed
azaleas soon to detonate in spring
when brooding hearts get flushed from their covers

MOVERS

We do need some, though fewer, of them—
these folks who crash into town presuming
you'll help with their piano, large appliances, crates.

Phineas (dashed by Zeus to blindness
for talk of coming things) warned
of their approaches from the south, counseled

daily stretching. On their travels, night and day,
Nature keeps at least an eye of flame or stone,
and both stare down in the wide postdawn

when U-Hauls back up a drive,
protrude their tongues of tempered steel.
Forget your plans to read or garden,

to steal the kids away for fishing—
there are dollies to maneuver, boxes to heft.
Fifteen decades back, in an unforeseen

explosion, the railway foreman Phineas Gage
had a tamping iron scream through his cheek,
exit the top of the skull. All Cavendish, Vermont,

was awed when Gage survived—returning,
in fact, to work a few months later (though not
his former self). Now that would make a fine excuse:

Metal . . . blown through face . . .
doctor says No lifting . . . Or simply:
I'd like to, but I'm not the person I was.

Who still believes we're haunted by anything more
than the darkling ghosts of each other's shadows?
Who wouldn't rather be taken for *granite,*

as freshmen sometimes type—for sturdy rock,
uncompromising boulder—than be obliged
to hoist a sleeper sofa two big flights?

Years ago, you strode in rain
through tumbles of newsprint on Pious Street.
Transvestites in their girl brawn offered tributes,

but you dreamed instead of country clubbers,
slim-souled, out yachting, of gold
afternoons stacked against the torpid.

Those were days of perfect freedom
and self-immolation, devoid of social duty,
hygiene—days, indeed, of acting like the second

Phineas Gage, *fitful, irreverent,*
and grossly profane, showing little deference
for his fellows. And those the nights

of dozing on ratty sofas, under stormy,
lightning-torn darkness, each flash
not unlike the visions of a prophet sightless.

Better start those deep knee bends. New neighbors
are arriving, with dining suites of walnut, bureaus massive
as caskets, blind promises of pizza and beer.

GENESIS OF HENRY MOORE

Mother's stare was stony
as any moon's. Now I paint
a river, and context is
what the water wants—
a boulder or two for scale.
Her eye was also cold,
and mothers' pasts go
best unsung. Already
I have finished the sky.
So be it: the clouds
are rags. I hear trickles
of crossing winds, glimpse
steelheads bent to spawn.
But when I brush,
the shapes won't stone.
Does an object create
the mind that names it?
Hereafter, my mind invents
what rocks it represents.

SUMMER PARTY WITHOUT MARK STRAND

> Wherever I am
> I am what is missing.
> —"KEEPING THINGS WHOLE"

Some arrive from the parched Midwest, others
on yachts christened *Shoals of Melancholy,*
Dissolving Messages, Sexual Pain. Still more
fly first class, gazing from windows at clouds
convoluted, gray as a brain. Strand's brain.

Syntaxes dizzy us, and we fail to devise
a love to tame them, which hardly fazes Dolores
beside the baby grand. Come in the name
of Cosmic Sorrow, she sips a sloe gin fizz,
waits for Strand to take the drink from her hand,

propose a dance. The marina winks.
Seagulls speak of an absolute largesse
stirring our hosts, drowning clocks,
and prompting a guest to flip through old LPs,
send Piaf through the wide French doors:

Non, je ne regrette rien . . . It's not too early,
nor too late, and we needn't choose between
the soft-spoken willows and blustering oaks,
since all trees belong, according to Strand,
to the same Franciscan order, attracting katydids, wrens,

and the fat raccoon a few kids, years ago,
dubbed Mark. Steamed littlenecks, barbecued corn.
Tiger lilies in a crystal vase. Too short and ugly
for Strand, a man stands in the hallway, considers
the skillful forgeries of mirrors. Running fingers

through bone-white hair, he inspects his teeth
for specks, wonders if his grin resembles Strand's—
coy, mildly sinister, like the smile on the side
of a jackknife blade. Now a one-book poet putters up
in a Nissan (get this) Stanza, whistling retardedly.

He extracts from his blazer lines in which he takes
exorbitant pride: "I consented to open / but you kept
folding / inward, like origami," and "The feeding owl
recalls a spinster / knitting a small gray cap." He has come
to share his craft with Strand of the perfect suit,

of crow's-feet spread like the former Japanese flag.
But where, after all, is Strand—to remind us
that the young are brash and temperamental
but their touch never a ruin? Who else will cut
through clinks of glass and silver to proclaim,

An unutterable loneliness springs from every hair
the philosopher splits? Yellow ball, red bikini,
wooden bowl of greens. *Remember me, M.S.?*
I was the twisted boy showered with stones.
I want to compose like the highway crow, swooping

at lulls in traffic to pick the mangled clean.
So waft appeals from greenhorns. And which of us
cannot imagine Strand's reply: *But really,*
what's the heart but a wry aside, set between
parentheses of ribs? How long has Dolores

dreamed of Strand, rolled inside her like a scroll?
Already, twilight tests the knobs of doors. Hammocks
of semidarkness sag between trees, and it seems
the far-off mountains finally might crash, like the freeze-frame
waves they are. Soon, a lovely storm will prance

on electric legs across the lawn. On cue of thunder,
I rise from the davenport and cry: *Mark, is that you,
old boy?*—forgetting that the thunder is Strand, the sky.
And in the bay, the names on hulls bob up and down:
Shadowy Flower, Blaze of Promise, Undeniable Selves.

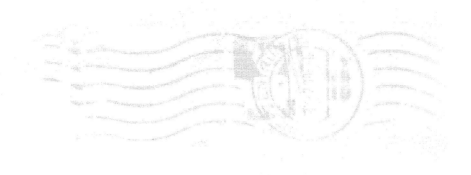

4

REVIEW OF *THE SELECTED WORKS OF STRAY DOG*

As soon as you encounter his brilliant opening
of trash, whiff the small hills of stool, once you wear
inside your eyes his eye whites pewter colored,
and paw the black grasses of night, you are bound
for the mausoleum of the visible. To follow Stray Dog
to the savings and loan, withdraw with him the vomit
deposited months before, is to understand
every yesterday sniffs at the carcass of this hour.
As Stray Dog declares: *Though stones do relish the state*
of surrender, casting ballots for one conservative
after the next, crabs—those first latitudinarians—
are easy in their shells, careful not to climb the ladder
the Renaissance made of nature. Then this:
The butcher is blue because the rabbit is small.
Too bad the butcher can't recall romping meadows,
the thousands of insects whiskers raised. Nowadays,
universities hold tag sales on landmark ideas.
Readers dutifully rummage through storms
in Stray Dog's fur, memorize the barks
swallowed after curses of passersby. The sky flew off
this morning—a huge balloon attached to the string
of collective awe. It left behind a father's shattered
artery, airports knotted in delay—lengthy ropes
of squandered time. Meanwhile, Stray Dog crouched,
collecting whispers: *mutt, filthy mongrel, cur.*

MILES

I piped the dizzy for who knows how, argued,
Without catacombs there can stand no town,
and one night slid my head through the crown
at church, then followed a river glued

to its ember. Who couldn't predict my brass
would one day burst? That I, end-time, would stew
in a velvet folly? A bashful kid, I consented to
spoil the mildew's nap, decapitate the grass,

haul trash to the curb in bags that were, after
transport, trash themselves. Never once did I aid
the roaches treated like thugs in black suede.
By travel, I hoped to find not heaven, but a rafter

where mind and body hang, negating one another.
No such. Wind combed back the cattails, I
turned in a circle that wouldn't point. Why decry
the addict, who only seeks a different bother?

Someplace florid, a prince paints a topical picture.
Imagine—art about actual happenings! Of course,
of course, of course, of course,
the unathletic started in: *Old world with your*

lovely clarities . . . Then I thought of the stars—
what trumpeted commotions fill their repertoires.

CANTICLES

I cannot translate the canticles of insects
but know what it means to love one's parents
only in their absence. Molting our mothers,

we wonder why fears spring most
on cloudless days, hear the old eccentric,
lost in her thunder box. Grown early

into queens and kings, we end as pawns,
bodies pushed toward bouquets.
I have tried in woman-time to mark the changes—

the must of a movie-house shutdown, an armchair's sheen
after vigorous dusting. Yet all the summers
seem blocked, while other seasons burnish

our faces. How was it the crumbs found me
in this green, white-toothed America?
How can the sun recline atop the morning

as if the native hadn't fathered the white man,
as if the nation weren't a patricide? An undertow
drags me back to lipstick, slender legs,

a parodic *Don't* the day I started a beard.
Who said, *There are seven knives in every woman,*
but one bread shared by many men?

In a park nearby, a saddled general poses
for a study in ambition. Cicadas choir
but can't inscribe. At least they fit their births.

SCURVY

I prefer to imagine sailors pre-1795,
before James Lind discovered the miracle of citrus.
Moved at the pace of salt, in defiance of far-flung heat,
they folded hands for hours of heroic boredom.

Dentin crumbled, bruises bloomed, rapiers of horizons clashed.
I too would sooner disappear into some blue distance
than reach for airy unknowns. The tragic shocks—
bleeding gums, spongy tissues—but also calms.

There are, in any event, smaller ways to live.
Flag these days, and the world sinks with you.
Meanwhile, English sailors are still called *limeys*—
lime once referring to both the green and yellow fruits.

JASON

Our work was vast, we needed barns
in which to sleep, cows (lovely atlases
on their sides) helping us plot course.

Today, in the public library of my name,
one great thinker scribbles fodder
for the next. I do not mock that august

edifice, nor the House of Suburbia,
safe in its grid. But when the patches
beneath my arms grow animal,

I know we've planted the darkest seeds
in each other's eyes. Why let
my forehead dam the rushes? Why

worry the past, as a tongue might do
a rotten molar? Nights, the old scars
open, call to one another—at 186,001 miles

per second. *Wake up, you fools,*
I nearly scream. *Hercules is mad.*
He thinks he knows the walleyed moon,

breathing twice per month through
crescent gills. Our only recourse now
is recollection: lithe spars lashed by rain,

the green last time we scoffed at hazards.
A false mind hides behind
my mind, a shadow brain

attempting its first full sentence.
Whose hand spoons this sugar, stirs up
Charybdis in a cup? In youth,

my good wife played the rock
to my sharpened scissors, clipped
paper dolls from every page I scrawled.

I covered the stone inside her chest.
But a man inhabits a city
then leaves so it may live in him.

Give me broken homes, sooner than those
that go on breaking. Hour by hour,
the bed-stand clock swallows rage, before

shrieking at six A.M. So this is what becomes
of pensioned swords, while in the breeze
one bamboo leaf sharpens the next.

JUST NOW

A redtail sprung and pinned a jay.
Robins—taunted day after day
by the muscle-heavy, black
and blue thug of a bird—squawked
in censure of the kill. Starlings,
wrens, and thrashers joined.
You'd think they'd sooner cheer,
given how the bully hoards
the seed we stock. Instead, the queer
collective drove at the captor's back.
The hawk regripped, double-checked
the weight to lift, then climbed—
the bruiser fussing in its hooks.
That's one way justice looks.

BEN'S APPLE

This morning while I read about Fallujah,
thirty dead, a good friend phones to say
her one-year-old can murmur *apple.*

I head out for the park, leaving the cat
at the window reciting her prayers,
but stop short on the porch, thinking

about my friend in her papered kitchen
holding up the deep red fruit
for her son to name, just as an Arab woman

sets milk in jars beside the oven
so the liquid bakes to a golden brown.
Apple, cries out a boy, as another war takes

blood samples in its search to find
a cure for life. *Apple,* he sings again,
and I hate my love of the sound.

With my shoe, I broom a pebble
into the yard. Blue sky branches
behind the trees. *Apple, apple,*

says Ben, as a distant woman runs
fingers through her boy's dark hair.
She cooks the almond cookies

called *ghorayebah,* apricot preserves.
Apricot: true translation
of forbidden fruit. What's safe?

To say I love my good friend more
than a soldier maimed, or stranger
pressing hands into sifted flour? To ask

how long a mother walks the seam
of a buried child? At my shoulder,
summer goes to seed, and Ben's apple

is delicious with annunciation.
I think of his open mouth—mostly
toothless—and step back inside.

UNMEMORIAM

We have failed to kneel for farm pigs
grasping life with bloody trotters, for rain
that hid in stone, buzzards haloing the gored.

I am not a prophet whose songs torment,
but I salute the hills just south of Dunkirk,
more wind-burned now than bandaged.

In defiance, British windows sang vibrato
to Nazi bombs. Time to praise the gargoyles
of Gdańsk, chips blown out of their faces.

Some days, the mind drops to the sternum,
stomach to foot soles, down to Nagasaki,
where plaques are nailed for shadows

photo-grafted to the pavement. How many
more reports of flesh unzipped
by shrapnel? Nothing comes of paeans

to the dead. One might as well lament
the trucks whose wheels came creaking
after moonlit sabotage. Somewhere,

friends raise glasses others will smash.
It won't be easy to persuade the solid women
reciting prayers into Sunday's horn,

but no more streamers, confetti parades.
All gods ripen and rot, and *History*
is a scholar's name for lost.

INTERNATIONAL TERMINAL

By now, twelve hours in flight, the reedy legs of my wife
knot with cramps. She must be trapped in a window seat,
beside a fat man snoring in Russian, hogging the armrest.

I name him Oleg, and decide he'll nearly die in his early fifties
on the floor of a hoagie shop in Narberth, clutching an arm
and whispering *uspakoisya* to calm himself as EMTs burst

on the scene. The one who resembles Mandelstam leans
close, greases the paddles that jolt, when three guys just out
of high school—crew cut, camouflaged, packed to fight—

march across my vision. I am ashamed in an airport café.
I have let my new wife travel alone, to witness a mother
and sisters cramped on Moscow's bleak east side,

and I have watched these soldiers pass without a word.
Who told me once, *There is no tenderness wrong*?
Who said, *A life can only plead for clemency*

on the strength of its latest kiss? Boys, where in hell
do you think you're going? I love you as I do the stars
unable to return affection—made like fathers to fire for ages

then implode. Come press dry lips to mine.
Wakeful as gods, we'll go down, with plenty of time.
The plane that carries my wife refuses to land, Oleg dreams

of picnics on a shore, of water's ruffled blanket under the sun,
and the death toll stands, this month alone, at 103.
Let's walk to the end of old friends' names, and find

they have no end. Dave Soley, Vince Cerio, Glen Griffith.
We were comets every one and golden—too young to take
our clunking hacks in Vietnam, too wispy and small

to copter in, and clutch the Mercury and Pluto of testicles,
scared beyond language, shit. Boys, you could have been us.
Timing, we know, is everything—everything but place.

Here, a doll with one lost eye appalls, or a doll asleep
with both eyes open. There, when night bombs rain,
you'll call for dark-haired *Mama,* pray for one thin root

in calmness. *Uspakoisya, uspakoisya.* At your age,
what did friends and I have to fear? Fathers, yes—
older brothers more. They loved us well at home,

but marched straight past at school. Our hands were theirs,
a family smell. Even the shirts on our backs were molted skins
of those dirty lizards. They swore they meant no harm,

then punched us in the common arm. Into whistle stones
we blew, into acorns' small berets—numberless sounds ago,
when travel meant vacation, troves of purple wampum,

abandoned tenements of horseshoe crabs. In green noons now,
I murder nothing, but cannot dream down graves,
whose headstones bob like flotsam of a crash at sea.

I love but never met you, younger brothers, and meet you here
at your *America,* whose word you'll keep if shrapnel finds a place.
A flight attendant whispers *Coffee?* She doesn't want to waken

Oleg, who envisions bright balloons (yellow, red), each flying
on one held breath. That's Afghanistan in flames, quilted
into mountain trees. Think cap guns, slingshots, M80s.

Think learner's permit, burning in your jeans, no cares except
not popping the clutch. Say prom. We graduated in '81,
after the Phils went all the way. Vietnam had faded,

and you three stayed unborn. That year, Oleg winced,
I can't feel my legs. Remember the deep, unspoken foam,
as does the sea. In waters cool, we douse the aches of limbs,

sanctify the newly born. My wife is coming home from home,
to weep about her mother's hands, folded at the kitchen table,
thin and slack as gloves. *Uspakoisya,* I will whisper, knowing

words change nothing but other words. *Calm down,* I'll say again,
as I did the day Dave Soley spread on an August hill.
The night before, his high-school-sweetheart wife went

down on another man, and drove right home to tell,
to sob and hold till dawn. That was the first time
Dave died. It takes practice before it sticks.

Sun and stone. Son and stone. Somewhere, rock unquarried
learns its alphabet and numbers, in preparation for my dates
and name. Learns slow, as granite should, so my wife

and I can sleep, side by side, beneath this nation's earth,
sharing an armrest of soil till the close of time. I used to hear
the recess bells. That me is gone. Still, boyhood friends

are home, tall inside as shadows late fall afternoons,
when we played touch until our mothers hollered *Dinner.*
I have little right to shout, and you're entitled to ignore.

I raise banners nonetheless of flesh undamaged,
and the mind is nurse. Like stone unhewn, I think and think
until the letters show: Oleg slender, Oleg lithe. He crouches,

cramps—his arced republic overhead, sickle in sight,
clicked inside the moon. He crawls the bottoms of dreams,
grubs for answers that won't exist. A robot voice calls *Moscow.*

I don't hear. The other patron in this night café
slathers lipstick till her mouth is a laceration. I don't see.
A metal hole starts spitting baggage. I don't care.

You're gone. Sky blue, sky stone. And Oleg sings alone:
*In flashes come the dead my brothers. We learned the honey talk
then ran through war to a blasted welcome. Home in Minsk,*

*I found a wife, curious and soft. She couldn't know the mime
bundled behind my brow. Out of our promise we climbed—
she alive, I alive, both of us dying of a former bond.*

*Full moons, with stone light, sharpened my business.
I cited frozen law in frozen words, grew the neck
of an owl to swivel neatly. With beak in back, I sensed*

*the elders, speaking platitudes with awful breath.
Surely, we share one memory, planted in our brains
before our brains. Whatever it might be, I still don't know.*

About the Author

Gregory Fraser is an associate professor of English at the University of West Georgia. His first book of poetry, *Strange Pietà,* won the Walt McDonald Poetry Prize and was a finalist for the Walt Whitman Award. A recipient of a grant from the National Endowment for the Arts, Fraser is the coauthor, with Chad Davidson, of the textbook *Writing Poetry: Creative and Critical Approaches*. He lives in Carrollton, Georgia.